This Song Writers Notebook Belongs To:

_____

Song Title:

Themes:

Lyrics

Notes:

Song Title:

Themes:

Lyrics

Notes:

Song Title:

Themes:

Lyrics

Notes:

Song Title:

Themes:

Lyrics

Notes:

Song Title:

Themes:

Lyrics

Notes:

Song Title:

Themes:

Lyrics

Notes:

Song Title:

Themes:

Lyrics

Notes:

Song Title:

Themes:

Lyrics

Notes:

Song Title:

Themes:

Lyrics

Notes:

Song Title:

Themes:

Lyrics

Notes:

Song Title:

Themes:

Lyrics

Notes:

Song Title:

Themes:

Lyrics

Notes:

Song Title:

Themes:

Lyrics

Notes:

Song Title:

Themes:

Lyrics

Notes:

Song Title:

Themes:

Lyrics

Notes:

Song Title:

Themes:

Lyrics

Notes:

Song Title:

Themes:

Lyrics

Notes:

Song Title:

Themes:

Lyrics

Notes:

Song Title:

Themes:

Lyrics

Notes:

Song Title:

Themes:

Lyrics

Notes:

Song Title:

Themes:

Lyrics

Notes:

Song Title:

Themes:

Lyrics

Notes:

Song Title:

Themes:

Lyrics

Notes:

Song Title:

Themes:

Lyrics

Notes:

Song Title:

Themes:

Lyrics

Notes:

Song Title:

Themes:

Lyrics

Notes:

Song Title:

Themes:

Lyrics

Notes:

Song Title:

Themes:

Lyrics

Notes:

Song Title:

Themes:

Lyrics

Notes:

Song Title:

Themes:

Lyrics

Notes:

Song Title:

Themes:

Lyrics

Notes:

Song Title:

Themes:

Lyrics

Notes:

Song Title:

Themes:

Lyrics

Notes:

Song Title:

Themes:

Lyrics

Notes:

Song Title:

Themes:

Lyrics

Notes:

Song Title:

Themes:

Lyrics

Notes:

Song Title:

Themes:

Lyrics

Notes:

Song Title:

Themes:

Lyrics

Notes:

Song Title:

Themes:

Lyrics

Notes:

Song Title:

Themes:

Lyrics

Notes:

Song Title:

Themes:

Lyrics

Notes:

Song Title:

Themes:

Lyrics

Notes:

Song Title:

Themes:

Lyrics

Notes:

Song Title:

Themes:

Lyrics

Notes:

Song Title:

Themes:

Lyrics

Notes:

Song Title:

Themes:

Lyrics

Notes:

Song Title:

Themes:

Lyrics

Notes:

Song Title:

Themes:

Lyrics

Notes:

Song Title:

Themes:

Lyrics

Notes:

Song Title:

Themes:

Lyrics

Notes:

Song Title:

Themes:

Lyrics

Notes:

Song Title:

Themes:

Lyrics

Notes:

Song Title:

Themes:

Lyrics

Notes:

Song Title:

Themes:

Lyrics

Notes:

Song Title:

Themes:

Lyrics

Notes:

Song Title:

Themes:

Lyrics

Notes:

Song Title:

Themes:

Lyrics

Notes:

Song Title:

Themes:

Lyrics

Notes:

Song Title:

Themes:

Lyrics

Notes:

CPSIA information can be obtained
at www.ICGtesting.com
Printed in the USA
LVHW012055141019
634127LV00007B/963/P